THE BATSFORD COLOUR BOOK OF HISTORIC RACING CARS

THE BATSFORD COLOUR BOOK OF
Historic Racing Cars
TO 1939

Introduction and commentaries by
Anthony Harding

B. T. BATSFORD LTD
LONDON & SYDNEY

First published 1975

Text © B. T. Batsford Ltd 1975

Filmset by Servis Filmsetting Ltd, Manchester
Printed and bound in Great Britain by
Morrison & Gibb Ltd, Edinburgh
for the publishers B. T. Batsford Ltd, 4 Fitzhardinge Street, London W1

ISBN 0 7134 3005 2

Contents

Author's Note

'The truth is never pure and rarely simple' – Oscar Wilde

An attempt to review nearly forty years of motor racing in 64 pages necessitates a very high compression ratio – time: words. The short Introduction is about racing at its highest level – Grand Prix racing – but it must be emphasised that all the time this was going on, other fields of motor sport were also flourishing alongside it – the voiturette class, track racing at Brooklands and elsewhere, hill-climbs and sprints, and, of course, record-breaking in its various categories. Shortage of space has precluded even the briefest of outlines of the frolics in these pastures. However, some pictures of a few of the cars actively engaged in them have purposely been included and the captions to these may help to tell a little of the story perhaps.

I am very grateful to those most stalwart of friends David Hodges, Denis Jenkinson and Cyril Posthumus, for picking the nits from the text and for the loan of some of the monochrome pictures.

Happy is the motoring scribbler today in the wealth of excellent, erudite and accurate books available to him from which to crib. I found the ones listed below first-rate for the purpose.

A.H.

A History of Motor Racing, Giovanni Lurani and David Hodges, Hamlyn, 1972
Power and Glory, William Court, Macdonald, 1966
Grand Prix Racing: Facts and Figures, George Monkhouse and Roland King-Farlow, Foulis, 1964
The Racing Car: Development and Design, C. Clutton, C. Posthumus and D. Jenkinson, Batsford, 1956
The Racing Car Pocketbook, Denis Jenkinson, Batsford, 1962
The Vintage Motor Car, Cecil Clutton and John Stanford, Batsford, 1954
The History of Brooklands Motor Course, William Boddy, Grenville, 1957
The Grand Prix Car, Laurence Pomeroy, Motor Racing Publications, 1949
Classic Cars in Profile, Profile Publications, 1966–1967
Cars in Profile: Collection One, Profile Publications, 1973
The Encyclopaedia of Motor Sport, G. N. Georgano (ed.), Ebury Press, 1971
Case History, Norman Smith, Autosport, 1958

6   (. . . and, of course, the invaluable *Motor Sport*)

Introduction

IN THE BEGINNING, 1894–1914

'There will always be someone ready to race something' – Denis Jenkinson

Getting off with a push-start, so to speak, when, how and why did the sport of motor-racing come about?

Karl Benz had his motor-cars going sufficiently well for them to be on sale to the public as early as 1888, and for a few years thereafter motoring around on your own in anything was regarded by the *cognoscenti* as a sport – while the uninitiated ranted about 'stinking rattletraps which scare the horses' of course – and, true, you did indeed have to be something of a sportsman to take up, and put up, with motoring at all as it was at the turn of the century.

But, homo sapiens being a competitive animal by nature, it wasn't long before one driver wanted to motor a bit faster than the other chap, and to prove that his horseless carriage would out-perform that of his rival – just as everyone had been doing *with* horses right back to the one-off Centaur Special of mythical fame – and thus was motor-racing born.

The very first organised motoring event came in 1894. It took the form of a reliability trial (rather than a race *per se*) over the 79 miles between Paris and Rouen, and the first arrival was the Comte Albert de Dion's steam-powered drag at 11.6 m.p.h.

The dates of 11/13 June 1895, are a landmark in motoring history, in that Emile Levassor's 4 h.p. twin-cylinder, tiller-steered Panhard-Levassor car won the first proper motor race. Twenty-two cars (15 petrol-, 6 steam-, 1 electric-driven) set out on a route Paris–Bordeaux–Paris, and nine of them completed the course with the indefatigable Levassor at the head. He drove, single-handed, for 48 hours 48 minutes, averaging 15 m.p.h. for the 732 miles – a motoring feat of endurance which must never be forgotten.

In late-Victorian and Edwardian times, France was undeniably the pre-eminent nation in the organisation of motoring competitions, and she also won the largest number of important ones – the firms of Panhard-Levassor and Peugeot being her most successful manufacturers. During the nine years 1895–1903 some scores of open road races were run, the most important of which were arranged by the Automobile Club de France and thus, naturally, started in Paris, usually finishing in another capital city but, now and then, calling for a return to base. The results table for the highest echelon of motor-racing of the day looks like this:

Year	Race	Distance	Driver	Speed
1895	Paris–Bordeaux–Paris	732 miles	E. Levassor (Panhard)	15.00 m.p.h.
1896	Paris–Marseilles–Paris	1063 miles	Mayade (Panhard)	15.70 m.p.h.
1898	Paris–Amsterdam–Paris	889 miles	F. Charron (Panhard)	26.90 m.p.h.
1899	Tour de France	1350 miles	R. de Knyff (Panhard)	30.20 m.p.h.
1900	Paris–Toulouse–Paris	837 miles	'Levegh' (Mors)	40.20 m.p.h.
1901	Paris–Berlin	687 miles	M. Fournier (Mors)	44.10 m.p.h.
1902	Paris–Vienna	615 miles	M. Renault (Renault)	38.90 m.p.h.
1903	Paris–Madrid	342 miles*	F. Gabriel (Mors)	65.30 m.p.h.

* Race stopped at Bordeaux.

. . . which just goes to show that (a) the early racing cars were quite fast and (b) that the old-time racing drivers and *mechaniciens* were tough – very tough – men, who put in mileages and hours at the wheels of intransigent cars in the most harrowing conditions of road and weather which would hardly be acceptable to the over-rewarded, over-publicised, pampered members of today's Grand Prix Drivers' Association . . . and without overtime pay either!

As ever, the drivers were a polyglot corps from several strata of the social scale, ranging from wealthy, but extremely competent, amateurs like the Baron de Caters, the Chevalier René de Knyff, the Hon. C. S. Rolls and the American, Foxhall Keene, through car manufacturers like Louis Renault, Emile Levassor and Alexandre Darracq and 'gentleman' motor-dealers such as Charles Jarrott and S. F. Edge, to works-employed test-drivers. Among the latter, for example, were Vincenzo Lancia (Fiat) and Francois Szisz (Renault), not forgetting a leavening of 'below-stairs' domestic staff represented by Count Florio's chauffeur Felice Nazzaro, who won more major races (four) than any other driver in the first eleven years of the new century. An amusing sidelight on the times is provided by the Olympian German Automobile Club, who were happy to allow Camille Jenatzy, a Belgian, to drive for Germany and Mercedes in Gordon Bennett races but who sorted the 'Gentlemen' from the 'Players' by ruling that the *nichthochgeboren* Mercedes test-drivers Braun and Werner must race as members of the 'Austrian' team – but still on Mercedes cars (built in Austria) of course!

Intrepid, trusting souls known as riding mechanics were usually carried to give notice of overtaking rivals, to pump up pressure in the fuel tanks, and to help wrestle new tyres on to fixed rims when the frequent punctures occurred (a dozen or more could be expected in the course of a race), though detachable rims were in general use by the 1907 Grand Prix.

Open-road racing went pretty well for a while, until – in 1903 – came the calamitous Paris to Madrid event, which was a disaster of a magnitude which, by the Grace of God, was not to recur for 52 years. So many were the accidents (a number of them fatal) to both competitors and spectators that the French Government ordered the abandonment of the race at Bordeaux, whither Fernand Gabriel's leading Mors had *averaged* 65.3 m.p.h. for 342 miles over narrow, pitted roads

8

which threw up such blinding clouds of dust that drivers, of necessity, conned their unstable mounts by taking bearings on the tops of the trees and telegraph poles which lined the route. This, of course, was thronged by uncontrolled and ignorant onlookers who were more accustomed to the passage and antics of horse-drawn vehicles than to racing cars capable of 90 m.p.h. . . . After the Paris–Madrid débâcle, motor races were run on closed circuits (though of considerable length) where adequate crowd control could be enforced.

We are mainly concerned here with the top class of racing, but voiturettes and 'light cars' were also competing in their own events at every stage. The front-rank racing cars of the early days had large, powerful engines built as lightly as possible (within the confines of materials and techniques available at that time) – or 'composed of air and optimism encased in the least possible thickness of metal' to quote the late Anthony Bird! These were placed in minimal, usually wooden, chassis, until the appearance in 1901 of the *avant-garde* Mercedes (itself a development of the 1899 Canstatt Daimler), with its pressed-steel frame, and whose 'modern' features – gate-change gearbox, honeycomb radiator – were widely copied by other manufacturers. Engines still remained large, however, and a dozen litres capacity was commonplace in racing cars (the 1905 Fiat managed 16.2 litres and the 1908 Daimler 17 litres) yet the weight of the cars was kept below the 1007 kg. (about a ton) top limit in force between 1902 and 1906. No wonder they went pretty well! However, as the years passed, engines became increasingly more efficient and thus capacities dropped, while more sophisticated chassis and running gear brought an increase in weight. The 1902 Panhard '70' for example, one of the most successful cars of its day, had a capacity of $13\frac{1}{2}$ litres and was capable of speeds of up to 90 m.p.h., while by 1908 the 12.8-litre Mercedes produced 120 b.h.p. and did 100 m.p.h. For 1914 came a limit of $4\frac{1}{2}$ litres on engines and the successful Mercedes had 115 b.h.p. and 110 m.p.h. on tap, with a weight of 1360 kg. (3000 lbs).

Edwardian international rivalry was provided by the Gordon Bennett races, held between 1900 and 1905, which were often run concurrently with other events, France winning four times out of six. The rules allowed a three-car team to each competing nation, which did not suit the French manufacturers – who outnumbered those of any other country, but were still only entitled to enter one team. Thus, when they had won the 1905 race and should therefore have been the organising hosts for 1906, they would have nothing to do with it (admittedly having given notice of their attitude before their 1905 victory). Instead the Automobile Club de France organised their first – *the* first – 'Grand Prix' to be run over 12 laps of a 64-mile course near Le Mans, and any number of manufacturers' teams could enter. A 13-litre Renault won. . . .

While, of course, there were other important races in the 1904–14 period, such as the Circuit des Ardennes, the RAC Tourist Trophy, the Kaiserpreiss, the Targa Florio and Vanderbilt Cup – plus the *Coupe de L'Auto* series for the

9

voiturette class – it was the French Grand Prix which carried the greatest acclaim and a victory was the goal of all racing-car manufacturers and drivers. It was run five times before war stopped play – three times by French cars (1906, Renault; 1912 and 1913, Peugeot), twice by German cars (1908 and 1914, Mercedes) and once by an Italian car (1907, Fiat). A month after Lautenschlager's Mercedes crossed the finishing line at Lyons to win the 1914 Grand Prix, the competing nations were at war and European racing came to a standstill.

The regulations which had governed the first 20 years of the sport were as follows:

1898   Weight limit: stripped cars to be over 400 kg.
1901   Weight limit: stripped cars to be over 650 kg.
1902/06 Maximum weight 1000 kg. (1007 with magneto)
1907   Fuel consumption limited to 9.4 m.p.g.
1908   Maximum piston area 117 sq. ins. = 155 mm. bore with 4 cylinders
1912   *Formule Libre*
1913   Fuel consumption limited to 14.1 m.p.g.
1914   Maximum capacity 4½ litres unsupercharged

FROM VINTAGE TO VANTAGE, 1919–1933

'O, for a draught of vintage! . . .' – John Keats

The 1919 Indianapolis 500 was the first important race to take place after the Armistice, and the Targa Florio was also run. These events were held again in 1920, but it was not until 1921 that Grand Prix racing was revived in Europe with the French GP, held once again at Le Mans. A 3-litre Formula was decided upon and straight-eight engines were the fashion of the day. The Ballot team were fancied to win, but the form was upset by America in the person of Jimmy Murphy, whose single o.h.c. Duesenberg employed hydraulic brakes for the first time on a Grand Prix car – the next All-American success was to be by Dan Gurney's Eagle in the Belgian GP of 1967! In September that year came the inauguration of the Italian GP, though but six cars ran, and this time Ballot got their own back and beat the Fiats – which didn't go down too well with the home crowd!

The Formula for the years 1922 to 1925 limited engine capacity to 2 litres with a minimum weight of 1433 lbs, which didn't make for very high performance in its initial stages – the 1922 cars were hard put to it to exceed 100 m.p.h. – but the use of superchargers soon improved matters and, by the end of the Formula, they were good for over 140 m.p.h. – and on stone-strewn surfaces and 400- to 500-mile courses, remember. . . .

1922 was the year of the 6-cylinder Fiat 804s, one of which won the French GP at Strasbourg from Bugatti (58 *minutes* behind!), France also being represented by Rolland-Pilain and Britain by Sunbeam and Aston Martin. They did it again on home ground, but against negligible opposition, in the extremely badly-supported Italian GP at the newly-opened Monza Autodrome. The following season was a much better one. The V-12 Delages appeared on the scene and Fiats came out with their excellent 8-cylinder supercharged 805s, which would have walked away with the French GP at Tours had not supercharger erosion put them out. The result was a British victory for Henry Segrave's Sunbeam which averaged 75.30 m.p.h. for 496 miles. At Monza, the 805s held up and came first and second, with 'that Yank' Jimmy Murphy third, this time on a Miller. This 1923 Italian GP saw the debut of the first German entry since the war, and also of the first-ever rear-engined Grand Prix car, combined in the smoothly aerodynamic shape of the prophetic, all-independently-sprung, twin o.h.c. 6-cylinder Benz *'tropfen-rennwagenen'* designed by the aeronautical engineer, Dr Rumpler. One of the team's drivers named Willi Walb was later to become racing director of Auto Union.

Once again the French GP at Lyons was the highlight of the 1924 season. The field of 22 cars included the new P2 Alfa Romeos, Bugatti Type 35s, Sunbeams now with superchargers – and the Fiat 805s of course. A magnificent tussle ended in a win for Campari's P2, with Delages second and third. Segrave (Sunbeam) was only fifth, but he was to win the Spanish GP, albeit without P2 opposition, but beating Mercedes, Delage and Bugatti all the same. It was to be the last GP victory by a British driver in a British car until 1955 (Brooks, Connaught, Syracuse GP).

No new cars appeared for 1925, but the V-12 Delages had acquired twin superchargers and produced 190 b.h.p. and 140 m.p.h., making them a close match for the P2 Alfas, exciting rivalry thus seeming assured. This was not to be, alas. Fiat eschewed racing for the season and Sunbeam were, by now, really out of the running. Delage met Alfa at Spa in Belgium, the latter winning at a canter before the former cars were properly sorted out mechanically – all three Delages retired. In the French GP at Montlhéry the Alfa team withdrew when Ascari was killed in an accident, leaving Delage an easy victory. In the Italian, Delage did not enter, leaving a virtual Alfa walk-over and – guess what? – Alfa left out the Spanish and Delage romped home! You scratch my back . . .?

The perennial Establishment apprehension that Grand Prix cars were going too quickly reared its head (with umpteen repetitions still to follow) and the capacity limit was reduced again, now to $1\frac{1}{2}$ litres, for 1926 and 1927, and throughout these two seasons entries generally were poor. The manufacturers were finding motor-racing over expensive for the return in publicity and sales. Fiat turned out once but Alfa backed out altogether, while only Talbots came from the Sunbeam–Talbot–Darracq organisation. Bugatti at last supercharged his cars and Delage introduced their wonderful blown straight-eight. During 1926 the latter had chassis problems and also tended to toast their drivers' trotters and accordingly they didn't have a very successful season which meant that, overall, it was a Bugatti year. 1927 was different however. The re-designed Delages (with 170 b.h.p.) came into their own and won all the four races for which they entered – the French, Spanish, Italian and British Grands Prix.

Although there were supposed to be some weight and fuel consumption restrictions (but none on engine capacity) most organisers ignored them during the years 1928 to 1930, and ran their events to *Formule Libre* which, surprisingly, failed to produce either decent fields or exciting racing. The P2 Alfas returned, but no new cars came out until the 2½-litre supercharged straight-eight Maserati of 1930, and meanwhile motor-racing was dominated by the Type 35 Bugattis, the *marque* winning more than half the 30 races contended over the three year period.

Despite *Formule Libre* the situation improved at the start of the new decade, and 1931 saw the debuts of the new Type 51, twin o.h.c., 2.27-litre supercharged Bugatti and the 2.3-litre 8-cylinder blown 'Monza' Alfa Romeo, which cars, with the 2½-litre Maseratis, alone made up the fields for the season. The three makes were pretty evenly matched on power, and again Bugatti was the most successful manufacturer. However, Vittorio Jano, of Alfa Romeo, had designed a new car which went much better than the 'Monza', and he had it ready for launching in June 1932. This was the immortal 2.6-litre Type B (or P3) *Monoposto* – a Grand Prix car of classical beauty (see page 52) and superb quality; it immediately won its first-ever race – the Italian GP fittingly – followed by the French, German and Monza GPs. Italy had replaced France as top-dog in Grand Prix racing.

Having proved their point, the Alfa Romeo Company withdrew their P3 cars for 1933 and left the Scuderia Ferrari to carry the banner by handing over the 'Monza' cars, now bored-out to 2.65 litres, for Enzo to race for them. But, as they were heavier by 200 kg. than the P3s they naturally didn't go as well and the 2.9 Maserati and Type 51 Bugatti won a few races again. Alfa riposted by getting out their P3s once more for Ferrari's team, who then went and won the Italian, Spanish and Czech Grands Prix plus some lesser events.

And that was to be the end of a motor-racing era. . . . A new, Teutonic technical autocracy was about to take over and sweep all before it.

DEUTSCHLAND ÜBER ALLES, 1934–1939

'The old order changeth, yielding place to new' – Alfred, Lord Tennyson

A new Grand Prix Formula, requiring a maximum weight of 750 kg. (15 cwt.) without fuel, water or tyres, and a minimum body width of 85 cm. (34 ins.) came into force for the 1934–1936 (later extended to 1937) seasons. Again the objective was to slow down the cars but, far from achieving it, the Formula spawned the most powerful and fastest machines which had been seen up to that time – and certainly one of the 'hairiest' Grand Prix cars of *all* time. These were the cataclysmic, magnificent Types W25 and W125 Mercedes-Benz and the rear-engined Types A and C Auto Unions, both teams certainly being partially subsidised by the Nazi government for propaganda purposes. Towards the end of the Formula, in 1937, both *marques* had cars with power/weight ratios of around 600 b.h.p. per ton and capable of speeds near to 200 m.p.h. The 1934 cars were the brilliant results of their designers being able to afford to start from scratch for the new specifications, whereas two of the Germans' major rivals – Alfa Romeo and Maserati – merely revised or modified their existing, pre-1934, cars to suit them.

Alfa Romeo thought they still had a Good Thing in the P3 and contented themselves with widening the bodywork to meet the requirement and boring-out its 8-cylinders a little to give 2.9 litres, while Maserati reckoned that their successful 2.9-litre car of 1933, with a widened chassis, was a fair enough bet for the time being. Bugatti, however, had done some re-thinking when the new Formula was announced in October 1932, and he came up with the aesthetically delightful, elegant, Type 59 (see page 50) which actually made its bow in the Czech GP of 1933 at 2.8 litres but now appeared enlarged to 3.3 litres for the new regulations – but, alas, to no great purpose, although it did win the Belgian GP of 1934 which the Germans did not contest.

One of the Wagnerian thunderbolts, the Mercedes-Benz, was of fairly conventional design. The engine of the W25 was a supercharged, twin o.h.c., straight-eight of 3360 ccs. producing some 350 b.h.p. at the outset in 1934, and the car had all-round independent suspension and hydraulic brakes. It was designed by Dr Hans Nibel. Conversely, the P-wagen Auto Union, designed by the great Dr Ferdinand Porsche, was very unusual, in that its single o.h.c., V-16 engine of 4360 ccs. (295 b.h.p.) was sited between the driver and the rear axle in a tubular chassis, which was also independently sprung by torsion bars at the front and swing axles aft.

In spite of their overwhelming superiority in performance, the new German GP cars were not yet entirely reliable, so they did not have things completely their own way in their first season, the Alfas managing to win the Monaco GP, the Avusrennen and the French GP. Nevertheless, Mercedes took the Eifelrennen, Coppa Acerbo and the Italian and Spanish Grands Prix while, for Auto Union, Hans Stuck won the German, Swiss and Czech GPs – the shape of things to come!

For 1935 Mercedes got 430 b.h.p. and Auto Union 375 b.h.p. from their respective engines and poor old Alfa, having already bored-out to 3.2 litres, could manage but 270, so, with the handling becoming very dodgy too, the P3's swansong was about to be croaked – but with a single, glorious, heroic exception. Tazio Nuvolari, in a special 3.8-litre P3 with Dubonnet i.f.s., beat the might of the Third Reich in its own Grand Prix by a superlative exhibition of driving brilliance and sheer guts. It was a great and famous victory. All the same, the Heavy Metal took every other major race of the season, the score at the end being Mercedes nine wins, Auto Union four.

Mercedes screwed 494 b.h.p. from their engine and also revised and shortened   13 their chassis for the 1936 version. Auto Union produced their C-type car, now up to 6 litres and producing 520 b.h.p. Of the Italians, only Alfa continued regularly to dispute the Grands Prix, with Maserati turning out occasionally but concentrating more and more upon the voiturette category. Bugatti confined himself to a single appearance and was completely outclassed. With the altered Mercedes chassis giving the drivers handling problems and some unreliability, it was Auto Union's season, with Bernd Rosemeyer winning five Grands Prix for them and Varzi one, against Rudolf Carraciola's two for Stuttgart. Nuvolari and Alfa *again* did them both in the Penya Rhin and Hungarian GPs!

Throughout 1937 Auto Union and Mercedes-Benz had things all their own way. The former left their successful C-type car more or less unchanged, but the Mercedes W125 was given a new tubular chassis, revised suspension and an engine increased in capacity to 5.6 litres and giving over 500 b.h.p. These cars would accelerate from rest to 140 m.p.h. in 11 seconds. . . . By the end of the season 646 b.h.p. at 5800 r.p.m. had been obtained from the M125 engine. Mercedes won seven Grands Prix and Auto Union five, and the only other team placed at all was Alfa with a single third.

Three litres supercharged or 4½ litres unblown, with some minimum weight stipulations depending on engine capacity, was the Formula which became law in 1938. Mercedes opted for a new V-12, 3-litre supercharged engine, which they placed in a chassis very similar, though lower, to that of the previous year's car, and enumerated the result the W154. Though less powerful (468 b.h.p.) than the W125 it was no slower round the circuits by virtue of its superior roadholding. Auto Union reduced their cylinders to twelve, in vee formation as before, with three camshafts and of three supercharged litres, while Alfa Romeo came out with three different engines – a V-16, and V-12 and an 8, all of three litres capacity and supercharged, but none of their outputs were anything like a match for those of the German cars. The French decided to play again with 4½-litre unblown cars from Talbot and Delahaye – having sulkily denigrated the French GP to the sports-car class for 1936 and '37 lest the Germans should win it . . . yet again. Maserati had a tentative go with their three-litre blown design, the 8CTF, which was fast enough to challenge the Nazis but far from reliable.

The 1938 and 1939 Grand Prix seasons were again Mercedes and Auto Union benefits, with the sole relief of the minor '38 Pau GP being won by Dreyfus, with Comotti third, both on Delahayes (and aided by a fall of snow!). The three-pointed star from Stuttgart was in ascendancy over the four rings from Zwickau, Mercedes winning 11 times to Auto Union's four. Alfa managed three second and three third places, Darracq two thirds and Maserati one third in the entire length of two full racing seasons. As Voltaire said 'God is always for the big battalions'.

But the nationality of the Big Battalions was about to be changed, on even more perilous fields of endeavour than the Grand Prix circuits, in the six years between 1939 and 1945 – and yet the flame survived.

The Plates

1902 TYPE Z MORS

The Societé d'Electrical et d'Automobiles Mors, of Paris, had considerable success in motor racing in the early years of the century.

For the 615 miles race from Paris to Vienna in 1902, Emile Mors prepared six 60 h.p. cars to be driven by the Hon. C. S. Rolls, the Baron de Caters, Henri Fournier, Fernand Gabriel and the Americans, William Vanderbilt and Foxhall Keene. Unfortunately, though they were good for around 80 m.p.h. flat out, all the cars crashed or retired from mechanical derangements, with the exception of de Caters who came ninth in the Heavy Class at 30.9 m.p.h.

These chain-driven cars had engines with four separate cylinders of 140 × 150 mm. giving a capacity of 9.2 litres, which were mounted in wooden chassis strengthened by steel flitch plates, and fitted with wooden wheels. A gilled-tube radiator was mounted low down in front of the 'coal-scuttle' bonnet.

This car, owned by W. D. S. Lake, is believed to be the one driven by de Caters. Bill Lake imported it back from the U.S.A. (in touring body form), whence it was sent in the early 'twenties and where it belonged to Mr Bendix of washing machine fame. It is almost certainly the only surviving racing car of its time in running order and original condition in England – and one of few in all Europe as well.

Photo: London Art Tech.

The Hon. Charles Rolls at the start of the 1902 Paris–Vienna.

1908 GRAND PRIX BENZ 120 H.P.

The German Benz Company built three cars to form the works team for the 1908 French Grand Prix at Dieppe, and this is one of them. The drivers were Victor Hémery, Réné Hanriot and Fritz Erle, who came second, third and seventh respectively – a very satisfactory result for a Company taking part in its first important race. The cars then went over to America, where Hémery again had some success (two second places) in the Savannah races of 1908 and 1910, and they were also driven by the redoubtable American, Barney Oldfield.

Two of the team are known to survive, and this is the one which was driven by Erle at Dieppe and which competed at Savannah. The o.h.v. engine has four cylinders cast in pairs (155 ×165 mm.) and a capacity of 12,400 ccs. There is a high tension magneto, a four-speed gearbox, and transmission is by side chains.

Photo: National Motor Museum

Erle's Benz, 1908 Grand Prix at Dieppe. (National Motor Museum).

1908 T. T. HUTTON

The so-called Hutton was really a four-cylinder Napier. It was built by the latter firm at a time when, hoist by their own earlier publicity pronouncements that six cylinders were obligatory for cars of more than about 12 h.p., the organisers of the 1908 Tourist Trophy race, which Napier wanted to win, decided that engines would be restricted to 25.6 h.p. measured by the recently inaurgurated RAC rating. Thus six cylinder piston diameters were too inefficient by 1908 standards to have any hope of success. The cars were named after J. E. Hutton, a car dealer who already marketed imported cars under his own name – a common practice of the day.

Thus three four-cylinder cars were built by Napier and entered in the T.T. under Mr Hutton's name. One of them, very ably driven by a Liverpool car dealer called William Watson, won the event at an average of 50.25 m.p.h. for 388 miles. This winning car is now owned, most appropriately, by Francis Hutton-Stott. The chassis is conventional for the time and the 4-cylinder engine has a swept volume of 5760 cc. (351.85 cu. in.) and a bore and stroke of 4 ×7 ins. (101.5 ×178 mm.) – the same bore was used by all the other competitors as well, which gave this T.T. its nickname of the 'Four Inch' race. The output is about 70 b.h.p. at 2000 r.p.m. and the car will proceed to nearly 80 m.p.h. with smoothness and flexibility.

Photo: Spencer Smith

Watson's car, 1908 Tourist Trophy.

1908 GRAND PRIX ITALA

This car was built by the Itala works at Turin, Italy, for the 480-mile French Grand Prix at Dieppe of 1908, where it was driven by Alessandro Cagno who finished in eleventh place.

The 12-litre engine has four cylinders (155 × 160 mm.) with overhead inlet and side exhaust valves and it produces 115/120 b.h.p. at 1600 r.p.m. The transmission, by open propeller shaft, is unusual at a time when most large racing cars employed chain drive.

The car was bought (for £35!) in 1936 by the well-known Vintagent Cecil Clutton who has been racing it ever since. Here he is seen in full cry at Shelsley Walsh hill-climb, and he has also lapped Brooklands in the Itala, with the present light touring body which replaced the racing body when the car was imported to England, at 101.8 m.p.h. In 1973 'Sam' Clutton and the Itala took the Edwardian record at Prescott hill-climb – in his twenty-fifth year of trying!

Photo: Robin Rew

Cagno's car before the 1908 Grand Prix. (National Motor Museum).

1912 GRAND PRIX LORRAINE-DIETRICH

This vast chain-driven Edwardian racing car, which is affectionately known as 'Vieux Charles Trois', is one of a team of four cars built by the De Dietrich works at Luneville in France especially for the 1912 French Grand Prix at Dieppe, which was run over two days. Three of them retired from the race with engine troubles on the first day, while the fourth car caught fire in the middle of the following night. . . .

Nevertheless, in spite of this poor showing, one of the cars was brought to this country by Sir Malcolm Campbell where it faired better than in its home land by scoring some successes at Brooklands, C. D. Wallbank taking several Class Records in the monster as late as 1929. It was also raced by A. Ellison and Douglas Hawkes.

The 4-cylinder, o.h.v. engine is over 15 litres with the very handsome bore and stroke of 155 ×200 mm. giving a capacity of 15,095 cc. Its half-acre or so of honeycomb radiator is decorated with a large, white Cross of Lorraine, and for some years R. G. J. Nash loaned it for display at Beaulieu.

Photo: National Motor Museum

Hanriot, 1912 French Grand Prix at Dieppe.

24

1912 'COUPE DE L'AUTO' SUNBEAM

Run concurrently with the 1912 French Grand Prix at Dieppe was the Voiturette or 'Light Car' (capacity limit 3 litres) race for the trophy presented by the motoring magazine *L'Auto* which was contested over 956 miles on two successive days.

The Sunbeam Motor Company, of Wolverhampton, entered four cars (plus a reserve) based on their touring 4-cylinder side-valve 12/16 model. The racing cars had bores and strokes of 80 × 149 mm. (2996 cc.) with semi-elliptic rear springs (as against ¾ elliptic) and a shorter wheelbase (8 ft. 11 in.) than that of the touring version. They were driven by Rigal, Resta, Caillois and Médinger. During the race, Resta was timed on the straight at 84.73 m.p.h. The first day's racing finished with Resta and Rigal leading Hancock's Vauxhall, who in turn was followed by Médinger – Caillois had retired. The second day saw the Sunbeams finish triumphantly in the first three places in the order Rigal, Resta and Médinger, the latter being no less than one hour and 40 minutes ahead of the fastest French competitor, a Th. Schneider. Victor Rigal's winning speed of 65.3 m.p.h. compared very favourably with the 68.45 m.p.h. of Boillot's 7.6-litre Peugeot which won the Grand Prix. . . .

Here a surviving 1912 team car is seen competing at Prescott hill-climb with Michael Ware, Curator of the National Motor Museum, at the wheel.

Photo: National Motor Museum

Dario Resta in the 1912 Grand Prix at Dieppe.

1914 GRAND PRIX MERCEDES

The 1914 French Grand Prix at Lyons was a classic race and the dramatic story of Georges Boillot's heroic but unsuccessful drive for Peugeot and La France, and the crushing 1–2–3 victory for the Wagnerian cohort from Mercedes and the Vaterland, has been told many times.

Mercedes built six cars specially for the race. They were driven by Christian Lautenschlager, who won at 65.35 m.p.h. for the 467 miles, Louis Wagner who was second and Otto Salzer who came third, while Max Sailer and T. Pilette both retired. The sixth car was a reserve.

The car opposite, which belongs to, and was restored by, Philip Mann, is Lautenschlager's winner, numbered II in the works team, and no. 28 in the race. The engine is a single o.h.c., four cylinder of 4½ litres (93 ×165 mm.) for which Mercedes claimed 115 b.h.p. The team cars were in advance of their time in most respects, apart from the braking system, and they had a maximum speed of around 112 m.p.h.

The mud wings were not fitted for the Grand Prix.

Photo: London Art Tech.

Lautenschlager at Lyons, 1914.

1922 DELAGE 'LA TORPILLE'

This car was built in 1922, and it was the first racing car to be made by the Delage works after the 1914–18 war. It was specifically built for hill-climbs and it had much success in this field at the well-known *venues* of the day, such as Mont Ventoux and La Turbie, in the hands of the leading French drivers René Thomas, Albert Divo and Robert Benoist. It has a pushrod o.h.v., six-cylinder engine of 80 × 150 mm. (5136 cc.).

In 1928 the car was purchased by Captain Alastair Miller, together with a similar-looking works car (though of 5.9 litres), and they were brought over to England, becoming known and entered at Brooklands as Delages II and I respectively, although the latter was of a later date than this one. Both of them were raced with much success at Brooklands by Miller and his nominated drivers, Delage II appearing there until 1932 after which it was re-bodied and used as a road car.

Its present owner, Nigel Arnold-Forster, has restored Delage II to its early Vintage guise, and he races it with great skill, *panache* and enthusiasm in Historic Racing Car events run by the Vintage Sports-Car Club of which he is the President.

Photo: Neill Bruce

Divo, Course de côte des 17 Tournants, *1925*.

1921/22 SUNBEAM 3-LITRE

With their big copper bolster fuel tanks, the racing Sunbeams of the early 'twenties look, perhaps, more Edwardian than Vintage, but under the bonnet the 3-litre twin o.h.c. straight-eight engine (65×112 mm. $= 2996$ cc.) was in the forefront of design for its day, giving 108 b.h.p. at 4000 r.p.m. and around 100 m.p.h.

This car, which belongs to Guy Shoosmith, was driven into fifth place in the 1921 Indianapolis 500 by an American, one Ora Haibe deputising for Dario Resta who was unable to start. On its return to Europe, Major Henry Segrave drove it in the 1921 French GP and also in the 1922 Tourist Trophy race. It finished ninth (and last) in the former event but in the 302 mile T.T. in the Isle of Man the following year, when the car was modified as to camshafts, carburetters and ignition arrangements, Segrave made fastest lap before he retired with magneto trouble shortly after half distance when leading the race. His team-mate Jean Chassagne went on to win in a sister car.

The car is at present on display at the Donington Collection.

Photo: Geoffrey Goddard

Segrave in practice, 1922 Tourist Trophy.

1922 GRAND PRIX ASTON MARTIN

The small British firm of Bamford & Martin Ltd, of Abingdon Road, Kensington, London, W.8, built two cars to take part in the 1922 French Grand Prix at Strasbourg, to be driven by Count Louis Zborowski and Colonel Clive Gallop. In the race, the former retired with a burnt-out armature and the latter when his magneto drive packed in.

The car illustrated (XL3125) was Colonel Gallop's, but, unfortunately, on the way home from Strasbourg it was very badly damaged in a road accident. It was rebuilt by the works and fitted with the engine from Zborowski's Grand Prix car and re-registered XP3037 in 1923. The engine is a twin o.h.c. 4-cylinder unit (65 × 112 mm.) of 1487 cc. which produced 55 b.h.p. at 4200 r.p.m. Top speed is about 105 m.p.h.

After its rebuild, the car subsequently came 2nd in the Penya Rhin GP at Barcelona driven by Zborowski, 3rd in the 1500 cc. race at Sitges, both in 1923, and it also had many Brooklands successes in the hands of Zborowski, Gallop and Captain A. G. Miller. Later well-known owners include F. E. Ellis, Commander Robert Hichens, D.S.O., D.S.C., R.N.V.R., and Mortimer Morris-Goodall. It now belongs to J. B. Emmott and is on loan to the National Motor Museum.

Photo: National Motor Museum

1922 French Grand Prix at Strasbourg; No. 8 Gallop, No. 15 Zborowski.

1924 ALFA ROMEO P2

Vittorio Jano (1891–1965) was undoubtedly the outstanding Italian automobile designer to date. His work included two landmarks in Grand Prix car design, the great Vintage and 1930s Alfa sports-cars and, after the war, the Lancia Aurelia GT series and the D24 and D50 Lancia competition cars.

The P2, Jano's first racing masterpiece, was introduced in 1924, and was immediately victorious in its first event, at Cremona, and also won the French and Italian Grands Prix of that year. It had a supercharged straight-eight engine of 2 litres capacity (61 × 85 mm.) which produced 134 b.h.p. at 5200 r.p.m., giving the P2 a top speed of about 135 m.p.h. It had a four-speed gearbox, magneto ignition and four-wheel brakes, and the whole was clothed in two-seater bodywork with a bull-nose radi-

ator cowl, though the latter was replaced by a flat squarish radiator for 1930.

These cars had a very successful career, winning nearly a score of major and lesser events, both as works cars and as the mounts of the Scuderia Ferrari drivers (see page 12) until 1930, when they were superceded by the P3 *monoposto*.

The original 1924 car illustrated is on show at the Alfa Romeo museum at Arese, outside Milan.

Photo: Alfa Romeo

Count Brilli-Peri, 1925 French Grand Prix at Montlhéry.

1925 SUNBEAM 'TIGER'

Although its V-12 engine is of only four litres capacity, the Sunbeam 'Tiger' has held both the World Land Speed Record and the Brooklands Outer Circuit Lap Record, as well as competing in road races and speed trials. The Land Speed Record was taken at 152.33 m.p.h. by Major (later Sir) Henry Segrave on Southport beach in 1926, and the Brooklands record went to Kaye Don at 137.58 m.p.h. in 1930.

The twin o.h.c. engine is based on two of the 1924 2-litre six-cylinder Sunbeam Grand Prix engines mounted in a 75 degree V on a special crankcase. With its Roots-type supercharger, it gave 306 b.h.p. at 5300 r.p.m. The chassis was an enlarged version of the GP car and was fitted with a two-seater body, the complete car weighing about 18 cwt.

This car, which is now owned by Neil Corner, was also raced by Sir Malcolm Campbell, and a sister car was built which was known as the 'Tigress'.

Photo: London Art Tech.

Segrave at the 1926 Spanish Grand Prix.

1926/36 DELAGE 1½-LITRE

The famous black Delage raced so successfully by Richard John Beattie Seaman during the 1936 season, when he beat the contemporary E.R.A.s and Maseratis in the Voiturette events driving a great, ten-year-old design with his accustomed natural brilliance.

The Delage was one of the cars originally built by the works for the 1½-litre Formula of 1926, and revised for 1927 (see page 11). The engine was a supercharged, twin o.h.c., straight eight (55.8 ×76 mm.) which, in 1927 form, gave 170 b.h.p. at 8000 r.p.m. and 130 m.p.h. In 1935 it was bought from Earl Howe by Dick Seaman, and substantially modified by the renowned ex-Alfa Romeo driver and mechanic Giulio Ramponi, with weight-saving particularly in mind. He did a grand job and, with an output up now to 185 b.h.p., 1936 was a very successful year for Seaman in which he won the RAC Light Car Race at Douglas, the Coppa Acerbo 1500 cc. race, the Prix de Berne and the 200 Miles Road Race at Donington Park. Dick's driving ability did not go un-noted either, and the following year he went to work for Mercedes-Benz.

The sable Delage was bought by Prince Chula Chakrabongse, for 'B.Bira' to drive, who modified again – this time with unsuccessful results. . . . During the war it was acquired by Reg. Parnell and thence passed into the hands of its present owner R. R. C. (Rob) Walker, who has restored it to as near 1936 condition as possible after vast vissicitudes. It is seen here adding distinction to the closing meeting of the Crystal Palace circuit in 1972.

Photo: Geoffrey Goddard

Dick Seaman, 1936 Isle of Man race, Douglas.

1930 BUGATTI TYPE 35

The over-worked adjective 'classic' must truly apply to the thoroughbred – or *Pur Sang* as they have it in Molsheim – Type 35 Bugatti. From its horse-shoe radiator to its knife-edge tail, it is a Grand Prix car of sound and purposeful proportions, and the esoteric eight-spoked aluminium wheels with their integral brake drums add something too.

The Type 35 series came in five versions, all of which looked alike and they also all had single overhead camshaft straight-eight engines with two-seater-width bodywork. They differed as follows:

1924   Type 35 2 litre unsupercharged (60 ×88 mm.).
1926   Type 35A, as 1924 but modified as to bore to 1½ litres (52 ×88 mm.).
1927   Type 35C, now a supercharged 2 litre (60 × 88 mm.).

1927   Type 35T, 2.3 litres unsupercharged (60 × 100 mm.).
1927   Type 35B, 2.3 litres supercharged (60 × 100 mm.).

The Type 35s were victorious as well as beautiful, and they won a lot of races for the Bugatti *Equipe* between 1924 and 1930 (see pages 12). This particularly well-preserved specimen belongs to the Meseu Do Automovel Do Caramulo in Portugal.

Photo: National Motor Museum

Garnier, 1924 French GP at Lyons.

1933 MASERATI 8CM

The 2.9-litre, twin o.h.c., supercharged straight-eight Maserati was 'more than a match for the Monza and P3 Alfa Romeos' according to George Monkhouse. It was to these cars that Tazio Nuvolari turned when he left Alfa Romeo in the middle of the 1933 season and drove as an 'independent' for the rest of that year and throughout 1934.

This car, which is part of the Donington Collection, is thought to be the second of Nuvolari's 2.9-litre Maseratis, built when the factory was selling many 'off-the-peg' GP contenders to private owners. It was on show at the Monza Autodrome Museum, outside Milan, before coming to England, and somewhere along the line it has acquired a Wilson pre-selector gearbox. The bore and stroke are 69 ×100 mm., which makes a swept volume of 2992 cc. and, with 10/12 lb./sq. in. boost, the output was claimed to be about 250 b.h.p. and top speed in the region of 145 m.p.h., though this would be without the additional weight of the pre-selector box.

Three of these cars were imported to Britain in the 'thirties and were raced successfully by Whitney Straight, Earl Howe, Prince 'Bira' and others.

Photo: Geoffrey Goddard

Zehender, 1935 French GP at Montlhéry.

44

1933 NAPIER-RAILTON

This is the only car in the book specifically built for track racing. It was designed by the famous Reid Railton, who at the time was Chief Engineer at Thomson & Taylor Ltd at Brooklands, for the wealthy fur broker and amateur racing driver, John Cobb.

The 24-litre Napier 'Lion' aero-engine has 12 cylinders in three banks of four – one bank is upright and the other two are at 60° to it. The bore and stroke are 139.7 ×130.2 mm. giving 23,970 cc. and an output of 502 b.h.p. at 2200 r.p.m. This is mounted in a sub-frame on a massive chassis which is underslung below the front and rear axles, with half elliptic springs for'ard and double-cantilever rear suspension.

The car first appeared in August, 1933, at Brooklands and competed there very successfully until 1937. It holds the Outer Circuit Lap Record in perpetuity at 143.44 m.p.h. It also won the 1935 B.R.D.C. 500 Mile and 1937 500 Kilometre races and took Long Distance records at Montlhéry track in 1933 and 1934, and at the Bonneville Salt Flats at Utah, U.S.A. in 1935 and 1936.

In the 1960s it was raced in Vintage Sports-Car Club events by the Hon. Patrick Lindsay, and it is now owned by T. A. Roberts.

Photo: Motor

John Cobb airborne at Brooklands.

1934 SIDE-VALVE AND 1936 O.H.C. AUSTIN 'SEVENS'

The blue car is the sole survivor of two side-valve 750 cc. racing cars built by the Austin Motor Company and raced successfully in road, track and sprint events, and in record-breaking, between 1933 and 1939. Early on they were driven by Pat Driscoll, Charlie Dodson and Charles Goodacre, and later by Bert Hadley and Mrs Kay Petre. With its Murray Jamieson supercharger, the little engine ran on a methanol/ethanol/water mixture and was said to be the most highly-developed side-valve unit ever to be made. It gave 54 b.h.p. at 5500 r.p.m., 69 b.h.p. at 6500 r.p.m. and 82 b.h.p. at 8000 r.p.m.

By 1936 Jamieson had his supercharged twin o.h.c. cars ready and these delightful-looking little scaled-down Grand Prix single-seaters were good for 9000 r.p.m.

and over 125 m.p.h. They were raced by the works up to 1939, driven by Dodson and Hadley, and were successful at Donington Park and Crystal Palace as well as in hill-climbs and at Brooklands. There are two survivors and here No. 10 is seen in 1939 form with barred radiator cowl and a central filler-cap.

Both these cars are on exhibition at the Donington Collection.

Photo: Geoffrey Goddard

Bira's side-valve, 1937 Nuffield Trophy; Hadley, 1939 twin o.h.c.

48

1934 BUGATTI TYPE 59

Ettore Bugatti (1881–1947) was trained as an artist and, as would be expected from such a designer, his racing cars number among the most beautiful ever to be built (see also page 42), whilst the Type 59 would be a high contender on anyone's short list for 'The Most Elegant Grand Prix Car' title! Unfortunately the Type 59, in Grand Prix racing, was not one of *Le Patron*'s most successful creations as it was designed for the 750 kilogramme Formula and it thus coincided with the technological onslaught from Mercedes-Benz and Auto Union, who were a bit much for an unsubsidised private manufacturer like Bugatti to take on in all conscience!

Nevertheless, the Type 59s had their moments in spite of everything – they came 1st and 2nd in the 1934 Belgian Grand Prix at Spa, driven by René Dreyfus and Antonio Brivio, in the absence of the German teams, while 3rd places came to Brivio, Dreyfus and Nuvolari in the Coppa Acerbo at Pescara, the Avus GP and the Spanish GP at San Sebastian respectively. In 1935 Jean-Pierre Wimille came 2nd in the Tunis Grand Prix. But the opposition was overwhelming and, while Bugattis turned out spasmodically in Grands Prix up to the war – but without much by way of success – Ettore concentrated his attentions on sports-car racing with excellent results.

The Type 59 has a supercharged twin o.h.c. straight-eight engine of 3257 cc. (72 × 100 mm.). The driver sits low down and alongside the propeller shaft in a two-seater-width cockpit . . . and note those delightful radially-spoked wheels, please!

Photo: National Motor Museum

René Dreyfus, 1934 Monaco GP, followed by Moll, Alfa Romeo P3.

1935 ALFA ROMEO TYPE B (P3)

Another great design from the board of Vittorio Jano, the P3 or *monoposto* was the car which brought Italy supremacy in Grand Prix racing in 1932 when Tazio Nuvolari and Rudolf Caracciola between them won four Grands Prix plus three other important races. A lot of victories followed in 1933 and 1934, and a few in 1935 and 1936 – though mainly in events which Mercedes-Benz and Auto Union did not dispute, but in an outstanding trio which they did (see page 14).

The fixed-head straight-eight engine has its cylinders arranged in two blocks of four, with twin overhead camshafts and twin superchargers, the capacity being increased for successive seasons – 1932/3: 2654 cc. (65 ×100 mm.); 1934/5: 2905 cc. (68 ×100 mm.); 1935: 3165 and 3822 cc. (71 ×100 mm. and 78 ×100 mm.). The respective power outputs were 1932/3: 215 b.h.p.; 1934: 255 b.h.p. and 1935: 265 and 330 b.h.p.

A unique feature of the design is the divided drive from a differential mounted on the rear of the gearbox by twin propeller shafts in torque tubes, one to each rear wheel.

The car illustrated was brought to England in 1936 by C. E. C. Martin who raced it as a private owner up to the war. It is now owned and raced by Robert Cooper.

Photo: Spencer Smith

Achille Varzi, 1934 Italian GP at Monza.

52

1935 FRAZER NASH

This is the first of three single-seaters built by A.F.N. Limited between 1935 and 1937. They were listed in the catalogue for sale to the public at £1050 ready to race, but there weren't many takers . . . most potential buyers opting for an E.R.A. The car was driven by A. F. P. Fane, with works collaboration, from 1936 until the end of the 1939 season.

The engine is a 4-cylinder, overhead camshaft, 1½-litre (69 × 100 mm.) unit with twin Centric superchargers. It was designed by Albert Gough of A.F.N. and it produces about 150 b.h.p. at 7000 r.p.m. The drive is taken to a countershaft, and thence to the rear axle by Duplex chains and sprockets in Proper Frazer Nash style. Maximum speed is about 125 m.p.h.

The cars had their successes, particularly in sprints and hill-climbs, Fane breaking Raymond Mays' E. R. A. Shelsley Walsh record in 1937 with a time of 38.77 seconds. His car was considerably modified in 1938/39, and it continued to be successful right up to the war.

This most attractive little car is now owned by John 'Jumbo' Goddard, who has loaned it for exhibition at the Donington Collection.

Photo: Geoffrey Goddard

Fane at Shelsley Walsh, 1939. (Louis Klemantaski).

1936 E.R.A. B-TYPE

Tuesday 22 May 1934 saw the debut at Brooklands of the E.R.A. voiturette at a time when a single-seater British road-racing car had not been seen for about seven years, and when one hadn't won a proper road race – as distinct from a track race – for an even longer period of time.

Raymond Mays, Peter Berthon and Humphrey Cook were responsible for English Racing Automobiles of Bourne in Lincolnshire, and their power-unit was based on the $1\frac{1}{2}$-litre, 6-cylinder Riley engine of the day, aided by an aluminium head and a supercharger designed by Tom Murray Jamieson. There were also cars with 1100 cc. and 2-litre versions of the engine. The chassis was designed by Reid Railton.

The E.R.A.s were extremely successful and they won many Continental voiturette races, thus upholding British prestige at a time when it was non-existent in the Grands Prix. Mays himself fittingly provided the first important E.R.A. victory in 1934 and Bob Gerard the last in 1950 – in between there were getting on for fifty others. . . . With the single exception which was written-off in a crash in 1936, all the pre-war E.R.A.s are still in existence today and most of them are still in active competition in Historic Racing Car events.

Here, in Prince Birabongse's Siamese racing colours, is 'Hanuman II' (R12B) which is owned by Bill Morris and David Kergon, and in the background is David Murray's R1A, the first car of the *marque* to be built.

Photo: Robin Rew

Prince Bira, 1938 Cork Grand Prix.

1934/37 M.G. MAGNETTE 'K3'

In the 1933 Mille Miglia, K3s entered by the M.G. Car Company of Abingdon-on-Thames came first and second in the 1100 cc. class and also won the Team Prize. The following year they attempted to repeat their success and entered three cars for the 1934 Mille Miglia, of which this is the only one which finished the race, being driven into second place in its class behind Piero Taruffi's Maserati by Count Giovanni Lurani and C. Penn-Hughes. In both these races the cars had 'square-rigged' two-seater sports-car bodies with slab tanks carrying the spare wheels.

The car was then bought by the famous record-breaker A. T. 'Goldie' Gardner, who in turn sold it to J. H. T. Smith who fitted a single-seater body in 1937, altering it later, and raced it at Donington Park and elsewhere up to the war.

The 6-cylinder single o.h.c. engine has a capacity of 1086 cc. (57 × 71 mm.) and a Roots-type Marshall supercharger and Wilson pre-selector gearbox are fitted. The output is 120 b.h.p. at 6500 r.p.m.

The 'K3' is now owned by Dudley Gahagen and it appears from time to time in V.S.C.C. events.

Photo: Neill Bruce

First monoposto body, Smith at Crystal Palace, 1938. (Louis Klemantaski).

1937 GRAND PRIX MERCEDES-BENZ W125

It is really almost incredible that an ex-works Mercedes-Benz W125 owned by a member should be crouched at bay in the paddock at a Vintage Silverstone Meeting. . . . Nevertheless here it is – the car most beautifully restored from the proverbial bag of bits by Colin Crabbe, and now owned by Neil Corner.

The W125 is the epitome of the fabulous 750 kilogramme (1934–37) cars. Its supercharged straight-eight, twin o.h.c. engine with four valves per cylinder, had a capacity of 5660 cc. (94 × 102 mm.). In a car weighing less than 15 cwt., it produced a maximum output of 646 b.h.p. and thus speeds approaching 200 m.p.h. on middle 1930s tyres, the W125 probably calling for more driving expertise to be successful – or just survive – than any GP car before or since. . . .

The supermen who drove the works team cars in the 1937 season were Hermann Lang, Rudolf Caracciola, Richard Seaman, Manfred von Brauchitsch, Christian Kautz and Geoffredo Zehender, and between them they won 6 first places, 9 second places and 6 thirds.

Neil Corner's splendid machine was used by von Brauchitsch in hill-climb events. In the course of restoration it has been necessary to give it a smaller supercharger than the Mercedes original, which proved to be beyond repair.

Photo: Geoffrey Goddard

Manfred von Brauchitsch, 1937 Donington GP.

1938 GRAND PRIX AUTO UNION

For the 3-litre supercharged/4½-litres unsupercharged Grand Prix Formula which came into force in 1938, Auto Union came out with a new car with a V-12 3-litre blown engine with three overhead camshafts, which produced 420 b.h.p., and de Dion rear suspension replaced the former swing axles. The cars had longer noses and the cockpits were considerably further aft than on the earlier cars. Top speed was about 185 m.p.h.

Here are some of the Auto Union team of four cars in the paddock at Berne before the 1938 Swiss Grand Prix. The drivers were Nuvolari, Stuck, Muller and Kautz. The race was won by Rudolf Caracciola (Mercedes), with Seaman and von Brauchitsch (Mercedes) second and third. Hans Stuck managed fourth place and Nuvolari 9th, the other two Auto Unions failing to complete the distance.

Note the detachable steering wheel in the cockpit of Nuvolari's car, No. 6.

Photo: National Motor Museum

Tazio Nuvolari, 1938 Swiss Grand Prix at Berne.